BREAKDOWN DANCER

BREAKDOWN DANCER

VIJAY R. NATHAN

Poets of Queens Press
New York, 2021

Designed and composed by Oleksandr Fraze-Frazenko.

ISBN: 978-1-7351478-4-0

The psychotic drowns in the same waters
in which the mystic swims with delight.
—*Psychology of the Future*

I say unto you: one must still have chaos in
oneself to be able to give birth to a dancing star.
—*Also Spoke Zarathustra*

CONTENTS

Anthem

My Prerogative
Bobby Brown

Poker Face
Lady Gaga

Killing Me Softly With His Song
Fugees

Crucify
Tori Amos

Stronger
The Score

Give Love
MC Yogi

I visit my past in dreams

where winds speak in rhyme;
such vivid colors appear,
query me: "Why, dear?"

Visions haunt me 'til my last.
searching for lost time.
This is the future I fear,
my mind never
                    clear

Once

Once I was born, crying and afraid.
Once I was let out into this world,
there was no turning back.
Once I lived in Great Kills, Staten Island.
Once I shrugged away from my mother
to see Tom, our neighbor, who built things
I needed to learn. He, the first guru
I followed, modeled being a man.
Once when my father tried to play
with me, his subtle resistance made me
understand what it means not to be
a child. Once our new puppy chewed
my toys so I no longer played as I once did.
Once as my sister approached the threshold
I shouted "Teenager!", cursing aging.
When she saw her first R rated movie,
my response was mixed with accusation
and jealousy. Once my first grade teacher
said she'd staple me to the chair. Once
we were all meant to fend for ourselves.
Once I wanted to grow up,
                              there was no turning back.
Now I have ventured into my primal artery
armed only with this poem, hoping
that this will be enough, and I will never
turn back.

An Indian-American Travels in Poland On a Night Train

Lady Gaga sings to me, *He can't read my poker face*
as we approach the restaurant car, our reflect-
ions floating in the windows of the night
train en route to Krakow, but Avi can
when he tells me,
                "You're not okay."
We navigate the train's sway, it rumbles
to its destination, we sit to drink
Blue Moons, I self-talk:
                Why can't I just calm down?

*

Those border agents make their way
to us, I say to Avi: "You're my Rock. I believe
there's a path for me, for us, to make
a difference in this tumultuous
Trump regime." Avi whispers:
"Perhaps the meds are no longer
effective, perhaps the illness has adjusted."

*

We split up, Avi left his passport in Warsaw.
The question lingers in the atmosphere: "Why did
they question us amongst those on the train?"

*

As I navigate Krakow alone, I rage
at the unfair night, going to the ER, where
they adjust my meds. I crush on nurse
practitioner who consoles me: "Everything is
going to be okay."

*

The next night I return, somehow tracing
my way back to that cutie, telling
her colleague I want to thank her
for her care, who tells me: "Oh, sorry,
my bad, she's not available."

*

Confused, my heart cracks
in the Polish nighttime heat.

*

I find myself in a Turon nightclub,
something about the sweetness of stripper,
who says: "I've never met a Black man before,"
compels me not to correct her.

*

Sometimes somethings are better
       to pass over in silence.

Who Am I? And Not Just That

I am grateful for this life, a balancing act
of a physical body whose sight
is a reflection of these images
from the past. I am this breath projection
on that razor's edge. I am a series
of information points. I am a son, a phantom
at a point of tension, so please give me
your attention. I am concentration, this wandering
cloud, an actor of muscles and nerves, a dancing
circle of blood. I don't know who I am. I conceive
of myself as a person, a human being, a meaningful
absence that is an empty space.
I am love, I am a lover, and I am loved.
There is frustration, introspection, and validation.
I am a yogi and a meditator that mediates
his interdependence, pivoting
like a boxer. I am a brother, an Indian-American, a man.
I am sexuality. I exist in your eyes. I am an occurrence
happening at the sound of a rumble, wherein
there is a trembling at the apex, our existence
as flexible as Indra's Net.

Love-lies-bleeding

The flower petal slips
            Sidewalk cracks / This
            Falling / Unawares
The spaces between.

"Come dig me up," the petal cries.
"You must find a way yourself," says his mother
"He will find the way himself," says his father

And then, the owl hoots. "Oh! flowers are so powerful!"
The pigeon coos. "Perhaps, but are they truthful?"
His mother and his father
dig and dig and dig.

When the sidewalk begins to seal,
creeping and crawling into itself,
the flower petal will not cry.

The wind will raise him
from those in-between spaces
to sing for his family:
            "This is a very nice day, a
        beautiful day…"

And the owl, the pigeon, the mother, the father,
and everything else dissolves
            "… the very most auspicious day
            of all…"
for the time being.

I Am the Ship You Built

You have had my blueprints
long before we met. These told you
how to build me from your longing

I am a vehicle that can bring you
to the places you want to be; I manifest
to gift you the experiences you crave.

You see me, allow me to emerge before you
on your perception waves,
                              only to sail your words,
carried away by your breath winds.

I occupy an empty-like
space to grasp at this body
you identified amongst the vast
e x p a n s e.

You were never content to see just anybody.

I am cast into your wine-dark sea;
your turbulent waters bestow
on me strength.

That is why you tear me apart every night
only to rebuild me every morning.

How to Unlock Your Heart in 8 Steps

1
Pluck your memories—
our past kaleidoscopic lives
are firm, mahogany cherries
at flavor peak.
2
Notice the bittersweetness
of these fruits that will grow
into the honorifics we mythologize
in our personhood.
3
Play table tennis,
so that you may know the score
is never predetermined, the operator
is not omniscient.
4
Ingest sacred honey
in your favorite mug, a safe
space where our trauma
began, sweeten naturally.
5
Build a city, not a dead city,
where cherry blossoms bloom
as a monument to living ones
we hold so dear.
6
The surface of the stars.
7
Straddle razor's edge
resting in intimate knowledge
of our lovers, strangers, enemies.
8
Forsake the sky;
release that which doesn't serve you
and allow it to rot
like cherries in barren soil.

Pradakshina

Summer vacation and I'm listless.
Thinking about starting middle school,
reading a book with waning interest.

A lone cyclist passes.

She circles the block,
again, and again, focused
on a pursuit of an unseen vision
of beauty.

I also want to enjoy the breeze
against my face, the cool
wind that channels her flowing locks.

I get my bike, wipe off the dust.

We catch up with each other. She's visiting
her cousin on Staten Island, she's restless,
long before the internet and smartphones.

Fearful when cars pass, I cut
the corner to the sidewalk, adjusting
my helmet as I hit every bump.

She rides the streets with ease,
without a care, or helmet, inspiring
me to overcome my fears and share
the road.

Although a mere 4 years my senior,
those impending years are vast.

She tells me she loves the green
parks in Virginia. I tell her
about *The Three Musketeers*.

It begins to drizzle.

My dad frantically waves
as I turn the block.
I steer to our driveway,
She passes me by.

I don't go home, but instead go
just once more around the block.

She is walking her bike inside.
She waves.
            The rain is coming down heavily now.

I don't see her the next day,
                        or any other.

Live my life in N.Y.C.

feelings must conceal.
Out of work by E.O.D.,
trying just to deal.

Cruising down the B.Q.E.,
awakened to the Real.
Bound towards the wine-dark sea,
To see what waves reveal

Masters of the Universe

After school he feels so dull

Until he couch jumps to soar

Holding up his plastic straw

Now he embodies this lore

He has the power to draw

The imagined Sword Grayskull.

Afro Avatar

A special pink sofa chair
in my childhood home
is an altar
to the image of a barefoot
clean shaven afro-man
in saffron robes—
                Sri Sathya Sai Baba
born 11.23.1926
dies Easter Sunday 2011.

In a frozen moment
my mother declares
she knows he is
              God.

She sees materializations
3 puffs of vibhuti
manifest from his empty hands
a sign of his Divinity

Others remains skeptical
seeing mere conjuring tricks.

At age 9, I receive His Holy Darshan,
visiting him in his abode Prasanti Nilayam, India.
I touch his feet when he waves his hands
to produces holy ash from
                      nothingness

When we accept a visitor in our home
who sits on the modest throne
reserved for Sathya Sai Baba's presence
in our home,
            a spell is broken

#NoFilter

We seek a rooftop bar
in Manhattan, when you say:
"We must go high… no…
… no…
                              Higher."
until we reach the midpoint
between here & the heavens.

Your finger traces the path to
the center of my bicep's
tattooed labyrinth. You say
"Well, that was easy!"

Later, I overhear a local say
"Good luck" to a Nigerian
who asks for the whereabouts
                    of the 'NYC skyline'.

Yes, I know the feeling
of being there, not seeing
what is all around you,
always forgetting
                    to look up.

The Place Where All Things Converge

Of what use is this Information Sciences degree
if not to to research how the lives
of our once-love progressed from the time
we knew them?

Yes, we confess we scour the internet
for news on our once-love. Pablo Neruda
was so right when he asserted *Love is so short,*
forgetting is so long.

We know so much more now
          about our once-love, more so
than we knew when we loved.

When we see their marriage is not ideal,
we wonder how other choices could have
had our fates entwined.

Sometimes, this cherry picking uncoils
Kundalini,
manifesting past apparitions, they appear
everywhere.

My once-love always gives me a cold,
quiet tsunami that jolts me awake.

This pain always follows that pleasure
as a shadow to the body.

Indoor voices

The couple standing
in line before me
speak so softly,

I wonder how
they even hear
each other.

What mysteries now
will never carry
crosswinds!

I seek to assure them
there is nothing
so grave.

Speak up, I shout:
your secrets are of no
interest to me!

All Possible Fates

Because she's not in love with me
I want to drown myself
in a fantasy that there is still
a chance for us to kiss
under the Bodhi tree.

Her erotic love is all I desire
for I cannot bear a life, this brief
incarnation, that doesn't contain
her intimacies, if only I were more
to her than an idiosyncrasy.

Please do not give me a lifetime
of this banal complacency
leaving my mind imagining: what if
I had chosen a different reality
that could have brought us together.

Yes, it's a fallacy to think an advanced
degree will give the understanding
that allows me to accept my life; my choices
are the key to all possible fates transforming
the unknown into my destiny.

The Anarchy Acrobats

A South Asian mother corners me
in a Barnes & Noble; her intention
is to introduce me to a nice woman.

I overhear the mother call
her daughter who is wandering
in the poetry section.

As the Mama narrates real time
location updates, they banter about
Dewey equivalencies they mistakenly
identify, to an audible gasp, as 363.4

I maneuver through the games,
employees shuffle customers
to leave, as several anarchists disrupt
closing procedures with a pyrotechnics display.

The daughter appears, her movements
still narrated over speaker-phone.

We see each other, the security gates close.

She cries: "How will I find you, my beloved?"
"Gmail me at truth to power show"!
Simultaneously, the anarchists ignite their own farts.

I am swept back into the store to another
exit, helplessly watching the duo cling
together, they are swept up as customers
swarm to seek escape.

My beloved shouts: "It's true. It's true,"
and I cry out: "No, no, it's 'truth'!"

The Lineage Transmissions

I endure endless car rides.

My inner realizations guide
surges of crackling
insight.

"Is it possible for me to achieve the Real?"

The author begins with cryptic
commentaries; perfunctory shorthand
within the margins of a leather bound book.

Light flashes from passing vehicles.
I study dense texts with notes
viewing them as lineage transmissions.

"Which color is my Death?"

Lines of escape always lead elsewhere.
The half-imaginary family dialectic is
[censored] only by being [unintelligible].

"Does this mean every person from
history calls themselves 'I'?"

For my drive doesn't lack
as my mind-drop ascends upwards
passing non-visible worlds.

"Why am I so thirsty?"

With no chance to quench
insistent need during
our long car ride, mother quips:

"Why not open the fridge
to drink the milk?"

Sungrazer Ode

Nothing purifies
quite like suffering—
joyfully liberating me
from erroneous beliefs.

While your tender embrace
heals, your pharmaceutical potions
cure me of psychosis.

Why, Logical Father? How,
Emotional Mother?

Uninvited Eros—
                    that bastard
is a troublesome meddler who birthes
the melancholy
                    plaguing your son.

Your Flower-Garland protects me
from future's harm,
            your Prismatic Compass
reveals the true north.

Where, Skillful Da? When, Intuitive Ma?

Divergent roads intersect—
not perfect, not sinful,
not reasonable,
not fearful.

As your son,
I'm not driven by any need
to delineate spaces
for your contestation—

My mere constellation
is some long forgotten space
from wherein I will radiate love.

Windy Hair

Clear skies
over Chicago
as we roam
the city
by tour bus.

Mother's hair
flies upwards,
her plump cheeks
aglow

Her smile mirrors
her 4-year-old son
whose multi-color
striped jacket
         expands.

Double-pony-tailed
9-year-old sister
stands aside
         with reserved smile

vigilant
         against the wind;
holding back.

The Pageant Marches On

Her body trembles, her softness has shifted:
a muscular tightening, a tectonic movement.
across endless note pages she scrawls:
om mani padme hum om mani padme hum om
mani padme hum
dedicates this to 'Liberation'.

Transverse sound waves trespass
invisible territories, she lingers in bed lost,
darkness embraces her, no longer clocking
time, the hours flow past. Somewhere else,
other families bathe in light to rejoice
in their fat and grow non virtuous.

Meanwhile, the unattended
water pot remains
at low simmer.

Everybody's Got Something to Hide Except Me and Nietzsche

Friedrich has traversed
the Martian landscape
on a Schwinn to say
                    "Blah, Blah, Blah."

He scribbles me alliterative aphorisms
he intends to be cryptic compliments,
such as:
            "Always allow your beauty to bloom."

Friedrich cranes his neck, gifts me
a Newton's cradle comprised of eight
of the nine planets.

Now, a fleeing philosopher, as evasive
as he is indirect, his moustache is coated
with chocolate milk.
                        Neptune sends
Mercury flying into retrograde as Friedrich
leans in, his eyes shut.

What My Body Knows

She writes: "Should I push you over the edge?
Or will you own your power?"

Body knows what body cannot process:
voice silently seals; beyond 'Yes' or 'No'.

The past rewrites. Silence underscores
quiet racing, breath expanding lungs
becoming air somewhere before my face.

When I am taught of intercourse,
I learn what bodies offer
when bodies entwine with other bodies,

I'm excited at the prospect of adult pleasures
awaiting me, but engulfed in my teenage libido
I consume this fire in my belly;
a beloved's whim triggers me to threaten
nonbeing.

Teach me this encoded blessing: I must
surrender
to Buddha; my body must cook
until it is burnt.

Patricia's Pill Palace

Insert, swallow, gulp! Now, away we go!
Deep in Poughkeepsie there's the strangest place
where Patricia brews up some magic drugs.
Now his high hopes for all humanity
are dashed against the best laid plans of thugs.
Is there nothing that can save our hero?
Our protagonist plans to overcome
all of Patricia's dirty schemes and work
and free the prisoners from her Ashram
wiping from her face that unholy smirk.
Forget all the arguments for free will;
Salvation reached in the will to power.
For it all began with a magic pill,
to be lost again in a whiskey sour.

Anthem

Beautiful Stranger
Madonna

You Dropped A Bomb On Me
The Gap Band

Love Yourself
Justin Beiber

You Spin Me Right Round
(Like A Record)
Top Of The Poppers

Never Gonna Give You Up
Rick Astley

Leather
Tori Amos

The Space Between Us

Always triggering those adjacent
        white motion-sensor lights

They monitor activity around
        dual remote-controlled garage-doors.

Never opening this black metal box
        with a silver handled lock.

I did not hear those sirens,
        didn't heed the approaching van.

Always those red-dotted lights circle
        a doorbell that connects vast distances.

You should understand the origins
        of the emotional currents at play.

Never will that red brick arch shrine
        contain your heart paper.

This series of tall, wavering shrubs
        forming a barrier between our lands.

Always this rectangular black tar driveway
        will connect all roads to your door.

I have traveled the vast territories between us
        and know the forces that drive us apart.

The Ashtray Serenades

That word 'Jessica' emerges
from the undifferentiated
scrawled somewhere.
               No, I think
as thought-chains tighten.

My friend assures me
"It wasn't the CIA who wrote
your first lover's name there,
so chill out."
               Sigh.

This tablet now appears
with inscription: A15.

That sense of control returns.

Acceptance floods impulses
 to investigate.

This past: a series of doors
slamming.

That not-looking; its own
glance backwards.

These neurons fire
as a way to heal.

That bowl, made of brass
and painted gold sings;
it is my makeshift ashtray.

Those cigarettes obscure
these Tibetan letters and images
I view it as holy and pure.

Sunlight Savings

Sometime between my birth and the present I stand at the entrance

to my childhood home I punch the door my fist

rapping against the wood My younger father opens an empty stare

He views my frozen upraised fist now a pointing finger I say

I am your future son here to warn you

about the consequences of your current actions. He steps aside,

allows me to enter Here illustrations of furniture

in empty rooms There a crude staircase image many

interceding walls with no enclosed rooms At the center

of this labyrinth is my mother who breastfeeds an infant I say

Do you know who I am? She: *You are the son of your mothe*

You are your father's child You are your sister's

brother In her arms only a space where I once was

My Pulse Races Into Unknown Futures

Over 20 years slip since we first met
making me wish our love was never so
Seek to kindle a past without regret
my feelings transmute an untimely glow
Another life, woven from this shame bark
invites me to live another truth path
why snuff out past love that arose on lark
whose erasure can merely seed a wrath
When divergent histories seem unreal
no intimacy woven that we've known
this ferments that hidden within love's seal
from veiled fields, propose memory unsown
Unravel quantum's thread these disapp years
to reveal the racing pulse loving rears

How I Overcame My Fear of Virginia Woolf
and Gained The Will to Power

The Stage Manager places left hand on her hips, shakes her head, then runs her right hand through her auburn hair, "Well, if you want to place a 1940s radio in a 1960s play, as the Director you can, but that's on you." I say, "Yeah, yeah." I tentatively pick up the old fashioned floor model radio sitting in the basement of the Cabaret Theater. It's heavy, a load to bear. "Can you help me bring this up to the stage?" She says, "I think you can handle that," She leaves me in the basement and walks upstairs towards the exit. I call out to her saying I would appreciate help. "It's a one-man job." The subject is closed. I tell myself, "I can handle this." My newfound willpower produces adrenaline. I'm hugging, squeezing eagerly, while placing stress on my back. "Goddamn it," I carry it as long as energy serves, navigating the twisting basement paths, and bearing my burden with a hardened smile. Was the stress on 'one' or 'man'? I wonder as I reach the threshold and begin to ascend. It's all about to slip out of my hands and fall down the stairs when I see in my mind's eye the future before me: I have already brought the set piece up the steps that lead to the landing before it turns to the right and then to the right again, forming an upwards U-turn, and I have positioned it as I wanted on the stage. I always have done it. Whenever I return to this moment, I hear myself reciting the same words, "This is my job."

Motel 6 Rendezvous

A Paradelle

We played endless online Scrabble games.
I was your only hope on the East Coast.
The sun was up at midnight in New Mexico.
No surprise; I was particularly good at screwing.
Midnight was screwing up New Mexico.
No sun was particularly a surprise.

The sun was up at midnight in New Mexico.
No surprise; I was particularly good at screwing.
You just like to swim around me.
Sometimes, I also enjoy going against protocol.
I also enjoy going around me, just like you
to sometimes swim against protocol.

You just like to swim around me.
Sometimes, I also enjoy going against protocol.
We played endless online Scrabble games.
I was your only hope on the East Coast.
Your only games are on endless hope; I was played.
We coast the East online.

We particularly played hope games, screwing protocol.
Enjoy the East Coast, just like me. Only you
swim against the endless New Mexico sun. I also
was up at midnight going around online.
Sometimes, your Scrabble was good, to no
surprise.

Viewing Marc Chagall's L'anniversaire

I am floating
as my woman trips
her back turns away
from my body.
But, wait!
       My neck twists
unnaturally. Although
I lacks arms,
             I'm relentless.
I close my eyes, purse my lips
and kiss her. Her eyes are agape
while her solitary arm
holds up flowers.

Above Us Only Sky

The doctors monitor the dreams
The doctors keep him under observation
His skin has the scars that cannot be explained
The scars are connected to the memory
He is not sure if the memories are real
Suspects the memories are of someone else
The dreams are about what's beyond skies above
About what's beneath soil
Momentarily, he gives up smoking cigarettes
Scribbles a poem on scrap paper
Far above are gas giants and darkness
Far below, fire and rock
Recalls the scribblings of the vagrant
Contemplates their imagined difference
He enjoys experiments with electricity
Far across the room sits the waiting mother
He enjoys eating ice cream with the mother
Just beneath the shirt is the scar
Watches as mother pours boiling water
He watches the father evade the strike
He remembers going fishing, catching Big Fish
He remembers joy, coupled with understanding
The road twists into the woods
The road never feels as it does today
The fish does not experience human feelings
Sometimes he does not experience feelings
He burns the poem in the drizzling rain
Lights the cigarette with the flames
The mother coughs, momentarily turns blue
Blue is the color of the Lord Krishna's skin
When he thinks back stories seem disconnected
As if the memory from the past life
The father maintains a close watch
The father is not ready to be alarmed
The past leaves a wondrous rainbow of scars
Professionals categorize the illness
The illness is something he cannot control

Waves pass through him
The currents flowing are peaceful
There is an ocean between him and the friends
These friends suffer, as he does, in their own way
These friends see him for what he is
In their own way, friends brag about the scars
In their own way, pain is the pride
The doctors will never release the diagnosis
The doctors disagree on the prognosis
When he pulls up the shirt to reveal the scar
The friends begin to rhythmically beat the chest
Now the gentle rains and the tears mix,
as water mixes with water.

This Is Not Not a Love Poem

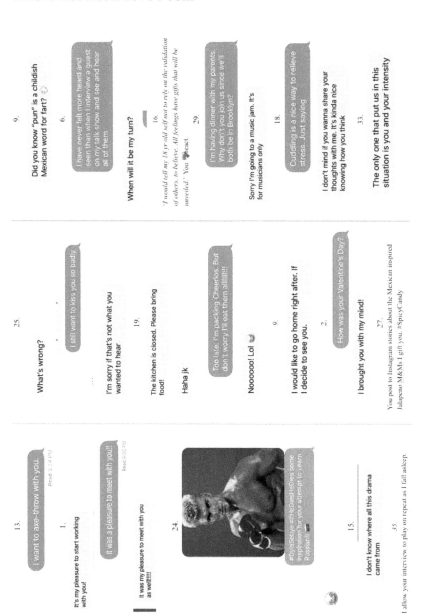

Breakdown dancer

1.
There is no single sound stage.

Many amateur dance troupes, such as
The Heartbreak Dishonors,
          and *Teenagers Disgraced*
form from an interplay
of psychiatrists, fairy dust,
and other imaginative failures.

This may be cash for those diagnosed:
                celebrity judges always
understand the choreography necessary to produce
delusions, so that all the high functioning
ballerinas can compulsively
              scapegoat their overly critical
social worker therapists.

Graduate fine arts students may compose
their thesis on breakdancing
deviations

this leads their psycho-
therapists to audition for
So You Think You Can Dance.

2.
I'm at the annual Vassar
'Homo Hop', walking alone,
shirtless.

        Up ahead is a student 'Hope'
who whispers for me to look:
          the girl I love has someone else's
hand up her skirt.

        I turn to see E wearing only

a towel. She points at me to say:
                                "You don't know me."

A 100K strong flash mob
begin to twerk in the space between us passing
by Sunset Lake,

leaving me to message about
its cold waters.
                                Send. Send.
                Send.

3.
King Claudius ushers me
to my seat for a performance
of *Whores, Bitches, and Crackheads.*

He whispers wordlessly this is
a reimagining of *Don Giovanni*

The stage manager reads the following:
                                "None of the
interpretative
dances are inspired by your personal history.
                                Most of the dances do
not mock your drunken mistakes. Please view
the show sanely."

The finale is a daisy chain of naked women kicking up
their heels to sing:
                "Such a perfect day, we're glad you
spent it with us.
        You just keep us hanging on."

4.
It has long been understood that manic-depressives run
in fancy panties.

Back up dancers who have a clever retort

to anxiety driven thoughts are more likely
to develop the 'Disquiet'

than are perfectionists who fail to start relay races
w. Personal Relic Hunters.

That choreographer who had sexual relations 20 yrs ago
with an unstable groupie that hoarded
10% of a disco ball
                    in her basement
has finally found himself...

                    ...in deep shit.

5.
An ambulance screams "Applesauce!
Applesauce!"

 I feverishly clap my hands.
The hospital's floor lights up as the music pumps.

I start to moonwalk.
The guard face punches me
in an attempt to bring me back to my senses.

The residents and the attending are conducting
a guerrilla Tai Chi battle.
Their mudras are diverse
and easily flowing.

A voice commands: "Finish him!"
and the credits abruptly roll.

Sacred Threads

From the Unreal lead me to the Real

A Black teen at the library says to me: "You don't seem like an Indian guy, you strike me as basically like a white dude."

At a library conference a white man purports to inform me that South Asians are basically Caucasian and that we're not of the Asian race.

My high school classmate on Staten Island genuinely asks if my family is from Italy justifying this to those present by saying "Hey, his family could be from Sicily".

From Darkness lead me into Light

When teaching a high school class I say to a student who asks if she could pass as South Asian: "I can see you killing it in a Bollywood film".

When traveling in India our guide translates for a local who says in Hindi, "He looks like one of us, but after he opens his mouth, we see his truth, an American". I blush.

For a period I've been fascinated by redheads, their freckled pale skin, who write to me on dating sites "I'm heading to India, any recs?" I respond with LMGTFY links.

From Death's grip, lead me to Immortality

I place 'Other' as my ethnicity. I no longer assert I'm Hindu, having laid claim as Western Buddhist, only to be commonly asked: "What's really the difference?"

My dad jokingly asserts that perhaps it was a waste to give me a sacred thread ceremony if it only took a decade for me to find a new path into Truth.

Om, shante, shante, shante.

Ah, A Pot Poem

I dream in color.   Indigo raindrops nosedive.   Blinking red hands bless.

Rocky Mountain echo.   He reserves the morning flight.   Indigo raindrops

nosedive.   Still water tastes carbonated.   Night before flight we

consume edibles.   When you see something.   Still water tastes carbonated.

Paralysis at crosswalk.   Say something.   Paralysis at crosswalk.

Rocky Mountain echo.   I dream in color.   Power walk to the airport.

Blinking red hands bless.

While I paraglide

I sing a song of old time
 whose meaning is rare
in these dark times of despair.
Turn away from me—
I brush against the sublime.
Flying on a dare
 singing: *Now I am aware.*

A Man For All Seasons

From my vantage point I can observe a man driving the leaves into a frenzied cyclone. The leaves billow before me. I feel some subtle connection to those leaves, as if my mind is the cause of their distress. Drivers pass my window in my field of vision, this is a quiet, peaceful block, except for the one man at war with the seasons. I can hear the phone ring. My cousin informs me planes have flown into the World Trade Center. The TV confirms. Yes, I know who is responsible for this event. Overwhelmed by regret,   I   confess the deed   to   an empty chair.   This is   the Holy war I
             once
idealized.   This past ripens, then   and now.   Christiana   Amanpour
hypothesizes on CNN, Osama Bin Laden   is hiding   in   a   villa   in
Pakistan,   I catch glimpses. My mind   wants to know   the truth.   Bin
Laden's shadow falls across   my path.
It's a delicate operation, uncovering   underlying   raging   doubts
 about our country.   A swarm of   psychiatrists cannot absolve me.   It is not
within   their rights.   My   choice of   the roast beef triggers
those
          series of events   leading   to Bin Laden's killing.
          Don't
verify for yourself.   My past   submerges.   While   others
 question   reality,   I choose.   "How do we know?" I scoff.   I know.

I know.   I know.   I know.   9.11   was   an   'inside'
job.
          Slippery
slopes   leading to the   Abyss.   Within it: History.   I   own
my own awakening.   Yes,   Yes,   I step into   my   power,
wearing my armor of Aripiprazole.   This   protects me.   The pinging
alerts me it's time   to   take   my pill   with   the
intention   to   transform my mind.   It's   a long road,
but   someday I'll   open   my
sesame.

This Little Dancing Flame of Mine

after Dylan Thomas

At the threshold age 18, I wanted to do
myself in, I regretted my love that did not
feel anything for me. I told them I could not go
on living. My body was fire, while still being gentle.
Psychiatrists swarmed to get me into
their care. I grudgingly went to groups that
shared their stories being prescribed wicked good
drugs that helped them to sleep at night.
As the years passed, I felt a rising of rage.
Though I didn't know the object of my rage,
I imagined myself on a battlefield, against
all those I hold close to my heart. This was the
fight I was assigned. Many times I was dying.
I trust that one day, armed with the blessings of
my circles of allies, I will allow myself to see the
truth: I have always been free to shine my Light.

Friendship Exchanges, Or The Sun, the Moon, and the Light

This is where the stars go when the Sun comes
Please just call me your rainmaker, baby
Our lives crossed paths as is orchestrated
We'll embark soon on the most epic quest
If we spend time together we'll transform
Friendship as precious as Rumi and Shams
Sometimes it's too easy to overthink
We observe our minds when we're together
It's never about us when you're with me
Divergent friendship like Rumi and Shams
After some time you abruptly transform
We have a quarrel as the Universe desired
Sometimes we wish our lives had never crossed
You're not my rainmaker, please don't call me
This is where the Sun goes when the stars come

For reasons unknown

inspiration manifests,
only to ensnare
phenomena that's nowhere.

My experience is sown
in empty conquests.
There must be freedom
This is my sacred wish.

Ho'oponopono

Occasionally your name appears
in my FB feed under memories, showing
you are not forgotten

Once, not so long ago, I used to talk
in an empty room, borderline mumbling,
as if that would organize my thoughts better

but I see you in that haze perhaps
reaching out in kinship although you may
not have been symptomatic, as I was

my diagnosis framed my recovery
perhaps your struggle lacked that scaffolding
which could have lead to your completion

I too, have thoughts of despair
they creep into the edges of me;
silence is the only appropriate response

I think about how you must have felt
when COVID lockdown hit
perhaps feeling more isolated than ever

when I'm alone, it's all I see
but I have already written the story
with no outlet, and so I will say:

their narrative is not mine to continue
their judgements are not mine to bear
their tragedies are not mine to reenact

when I talk to my cat today I see only
pure being, raw instinct, her honed reflex
to survive, rotating her body as she falls

My heart goes out to the spaces
which manifests whenever you arise
when I recite this prayer, hoping you will hear:

I'm sorry, please forgive me,
I thank you for being my friend,
I love you, and I love myself.

Now Is The Time

Now, I say: "I'm a great supervisor."
We wait for that Vampire Weekend concert.

"This country is lost."
We walk in these Manhattan streets.

"This country needs true leadership."
We look for a less crowded restaurant.
"The world is about to change."

He's frightened for me, or perhaps of me?
Now, he says, "I don't want to go to the concert."
I say: "I need to go home."

I venture towards the subway, but he follows me,
because he loves me. I cannot shake him,
although he seems shook.

Now, I say: "I've been asleep for so long."
"Jesus has stirred my life. I need you to believe."
Now, he says: "This, too, shall pass."

We have plans. Now, they fall away. We have plans.
Now, they seem so distant. We have plans. Now, they
are cancelled. We have plans. Now, they are not essential.
We have plans.

So, too, does the Lord.

This Body is a Garden

There are perennials growing in my perineum.

There are roses crowding up my brain.

The lilies entwine with my chest hair,

leaving my hands tied up in a daisy chain.

While daffodils multiply in my bowels,

the tomatoes are plucked ripe from my spine.

Asparagus is growing from my testes

above legs of corn stalks harvested in a line.

Alms Rounds in Fang Valley

Slippers hit the ground
       Slap!
I follow the Buddhist Monks
as we walk down the small road, heads
bowed, deep in contemplation
Slap! *Slap!*
         Connecting with the main
street, leading to the market.
Quiet steps. Mindfulness.

Thoughts arise in my mind
guided by the walking
meditation:
Right goes thus,
left goes thus,
right goes thus,
left goes thus.

The memory of a military
march arises: Left! Left!
Left, Right, Left!
I just note: daydreaming, daydreaming, and bring
my attention back
to the right and the left
as they go thus.

The morning light
arrives as we walk towards
the marketplace.

Along the way the locals offer
the monks food and in return
the monks give
a blessing.

Sphinx of Black Quartz, Judge my Vow

We are permitted
to relax, to allow
openness
in our chest & lungs.

We will feel
the energy released
in our Anahata chakra.

Our heart center: a redness
a sacred scarlet phenomena
a double tetrahedron exits
the center of a mandala

taking the image
of a celestial moon,
pale, full, hanging
                    The darkness of the night.

The meditation industry stretches
across civilizations, hits
the American mainstream culture
as a way to cope.

Know these button-shaped meditation
cushions are perfect
            for our developing
or established practice.
                    Take a moment to be.

Whether we're in the habit of a daily sit
or want to commit to an easy
reflection routine, these products support
even the most intense austerities.

Mindfulness training makes up 7.4 percent
of the $15.1 billion alternative

care market, a $1.1 billion industry
in the United States.

Companies hold out arms
         embracing us as we arise.
Take all the time you need.

We sit in an elevated cross leg
or lotus posture, to discover
the cushion that creates
pelvic tilt, bringing alignment.

These button shaped cushions
are available in an array of colors:
'sage green', 'burgundy', 'navy blue', 'lilac',
'steel blue', and
                 The color of endless sand dropping
within the hourglass, milestones
on our life-journey, passing
                 its narrow, narrow neck.

Anthem

When Doves Cry
Prince

Crazy
Gnarls Barkley

Bad Case of Loving you
(Doctor Doctor)
Robert Palmer

Hold it against me
Britney Spears

I Touch Myself
Divinyls

You Get What You Give
New Radicals

About the Author

VIJAY R. NATHAN is a librarian in New York City. He hosts the live talk show *The Truth to Power Show* that streams on Radio Free Brooklyn's internet platform and apps. With his published works, he seeks to create a sacred space, both for his own process, and, with *Nine Cloud Journal*, for the processes of his community to share their stories of truth and empowerment. He wishes for you to enjoy resonances with his journey and thanks you for your kind time spent sitting with his poems and listening to the playlists.
Find out more at: https://vijayrnathan.com

Acknowledgements

"Everyone's Got Something To Hide Except Me and Nietzsche" was first published online by *Meow Meow Pow Pow Lit* February 2019 and was nominated for the Pushcart Prize 2019.
"The Lineage Annotations" (now published as 'The Lineage Transmissions') was first published online by *Showbear Family Circus* June 2019.
"Love-Lies-Bleeding" and "Sphinx of Black Quartz, Judge My Vow" was first published by *Newtown Literary*, Spring 2019 (Issue 13).
"Breakdown Dancer" was first published in *Fearsome Critters* May 2019 (Volume 2).
"That Holy Singing Ashtray" (now "The Ashtray Serenades"), "Pradakshina", and "#NoFilter" were published in *Poets of Queens* anthology Summer 2020.
"Motel 6 Rendezvous" was first published in *High Shelf Magazine* July 2020 (Issue XX).
"Windy Hair" and "Sunlight Savings" were first published online at *Ducts.org* in Summer 2019 (Issue 42).
"Above Us Only Sky" and "Adieu Haiku" (Live my life in NYC) was first published in *Nine Cloud Journal* in August 2020 (Issue 1). "An Indian American Travels in Poland on a Night Train" first appeared in *Nine Cloud Journal* in May 2021 (Issue 2).
A variation on "Above Us Only Sky" was republished by *Closed Eye Open* online journal (Issue 2, 2020).
"Sacred Threads" was first published by *iO Journal* in (Issue 3, 2021).
"Friendship Exchanges, Or the Sun, the Moon, and the Light" and "Alms Round in Fang Valley" were first published with Spoke Magazine (Issue 8, 2021)

Thanks to *Brooklyn Poets* for their classes where many of the draft poems were workshopped. Specifically, Vanessa Jimenez Gabb for the class "The Modern (Anti-) Love Poem" (and comments on the manuscript), Jason Koo for the class "Fast Break: Capturing the Motion of the Mind", and Xan Phillips for the class "Feeding Yourself". Thanks to Bianca Stone and Rosebud Ben-Oni for feedback on selected poems.

Thanks to my encouraging friends and beta readers. Very special thanks to Claire Van Winkle of *Rockaway Writers Workshop* (and the associated writers) for intensive feedback.

Prior Works

Escape from Samsara: Poems (2016)

Celebrity Sadhana, Or How to Meditate with a Hammer
The Paparazzo Poet Meditations, Book 1 (2018)

·

CPSIA information can be obtained
at www.ICGtesting.com
Printed in the USA
LVHW081215110222
710664LV00003B/110